Kyle's Attic

by Debbie Shapiro
illustrated by Dona Turner

Orlando Boston Dallas Chicago San Diego

Visit *The Learning Site!*

www.harcourtschool.com

Kyle was sad because no one could come and play. He wanted to do something to cheer up.

2

"I know! I'll go into the attic.
I love the attic because there
are lots of surprises there."

Kyle opened the creaky door.
The attic was dark and dusty.
Old things were piled up high.

4

"My! Look at everything!"
Kyle cried. "This is fun!"
First he opened an old chest.

5

Then he opened a box. He
wanted to know if the dolls
had been his mother's.

"My, my!" Kyle saw old
baseballs, skates, and a bike.
Kyle could try them in the
backyard.

A pretty box on a high shelf
had plenty of old pictures in
it. Kyle loved looking at them
again and again.

Then Kyle saw a soft bear that his Dad had played with when he was small. It had a big blue bow on it.

Kyle found something special,
so he took the old bear and
left the attic.

10

"Mom, would you give us
some pie and then sing us
a lullaby?" Kyle asked.

"I love my new friend."
Kyle made a new friend
on a stormy day.